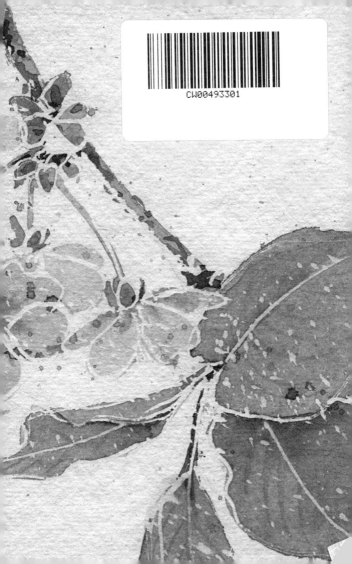

CW00493301

Herbal Chronicles

Healing herbs from the hedgerow

Sarah Atkinson
Medical Herbalist
Sally Bamber
Designer Artist

First published in 2021 By Sarah Atkinson
Orchard Head, Foxfield, Broughton-in-Furness
Cumbria LA20 6BT

Watercolours by Sally Bamber
Designed & produced by Sally Bamber
www.sallybamber.com

Printed by Beam Reach Printing
www.beamreachuk.co.uk

Further copies of this book may be obtained from
Sarah Atkinson – sarah.atkinson4941@live.co.uk
Sally Bamber – hello@sallybamber.com

ISBN 978-1-5272-8936-9

Contents

Herbal terms

Tincture

An alcoholic extract made by infusing a herb in an alcohol solution for a minimum of two weeks. After this time it's strained and bottled – this method allows any non water-soluble elements to be dissolved and made available in the tincture, also the alcohol acts as a preservative.

Tea

The herb, either fresh or dried, is placed into boiling water and allowed to stand for four-five minutes before straining and drinking.

Decoction

This is used for woody herbs – the bark or roots are simmered in water for around 10 minutes before the mixture is strained and drunk.

Class 20

A herb that is deemed to be Class 20 has very restricted uses and can only be prescribed by a fully qualified herbalist. These herbs definitely should not be used for self medication.

Coughs and colds

Plantain
Plantago lanceolata/Plantago major

The leaves of this very common herb come in two
varieties – *lanceolata* are long and thin, like a lance,
while the leaves of the *major* are larger and more
rounded. They both have distinct ribs on the back
of the leaves, hence the common name ribwort.

This herb contains high levels of zinc which makes
it very healing for cuts and grazes as well as useful
in treating coughs. But its main effect is on mucous
membranes – our bodies produce mucus to protect
us from irritation but sometimes the mucus becomes
the problem.

A couple of years ago I was visiting some friends
whose daughter had just had her jaw realigned – I
didn't see her during our visit but my friend reported
that her daughter's entire face was covered in
bandages and she could only take in sustenance and
fluids through a straw. Soon it became clear that due to
the surgery a lot of mucus was being produced and this
girl was struggling to swallow and breathe easily. I
suggested that we went for a walk in their garden and
immediately I saw that her lawn had an abundance of
plantain – we gathered a handful and made a tea out

of it. The result was surprisingly fast – the mucus began to reduce and our friend's daughter was more comfortable by the next day.

It's easy to assume that because herbs are 'natural' they can only work slowly – this may be the case but not always. We were told during my time at the School of Phytotherapy that we should allow one month's treatment for each year that a condition has been present. In my experience this is a useful guide but in addition to this I have noticed that if someone is fundamentally well and happy, they will get better quickly.

Ground Ivy
Glechoma hederacea

A small, creeping spring herb with furry leaves and tiny blue flowers.

Glecoma hederacea can be made into a mucous membrane tonic – toning the mucous membranes so that they don't need to overproduce mucus, similar in action to plantain.

I will always remember a very well-respected herbalist Christopher Hedley – who sadly died in 2017 – talking about his dispensary and how he had decided to label ground ivy as Ale Hoof, its Anglo-Saxon name, much to the confusion of the students who trained with him.

The Anglo Saxons used ground ivy to flavour beer – it has a very distinctive and bitter aroma. I mentioned this to my son who has a microbrewery and he said that there were very good reasons for using hops in more modern beers where they act as both a flavouring and a preservative. Ale Hoof's flavour and preservative qualities don't quite match up to that of the hop. Ground ivy is an excellent tonic, regardless.

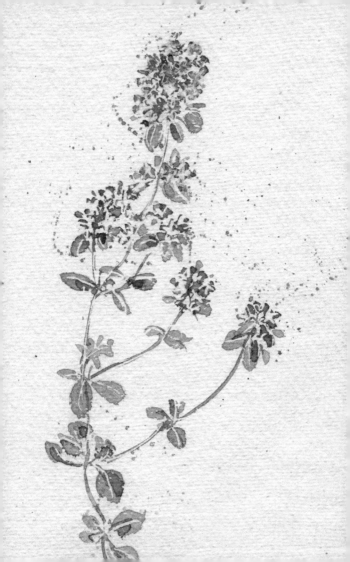

Thyme
Thymus vulgaris

Thyme is a fragrant Mediterranean herb with tiny purple flowers much loved by bees. It is harvested when it is in flower and, although wild thyme grows on the fells around here, I haven't managed to grow it successfully in my garden where it's too wet and cold for thyme.

The two main essential oils which make up the smell of thyme are thymol and carvacrol – these are both antimicrobial and are very useful in treating chest infections. Essential oils can diffuse through tissue which means that taking thyme as a drink enables the oils to also diffuse into the lungs, allowing the antimicrobial effect to reach the source of infection.

Thyme has other beneficial effects on upper respiratory infections – it thins mucus making it less sticky and stimulates the 'muco-ciliary escalator' thereby allowing mucus to be coughed up easily.

Thyme can also be used for its urinary antimicrobial effect but the carvacrol element can be irritating to the kidneys. I use it carefully and case by case in this instance.

Coltsfoot
Tussilago farfara

Both leaves and flowers are used. The flowers bloom before the leaves develop in early spring – they look like low growing dandelions with smaller flower heads.

The flowers can be boiled with sugar to make a soothing cough syrup.

The leaves are distinctive in appearance because they look as though they are covered in cobwebs – a covering that can be easily wiped off.

I have used coltsfoot leaf tincture for many years; as my starting point for treating any lung condition; it's high in zinc which encourages tissue healing. Also, it has a soothing effect on the respiratory system which reduces cattarrh and inflammation and eases irritating coughs.

The leaves used to be the basis for herbal tobacco – they tend to smoulder which makes the mixture behave more like a conventional tobacco. The idea of smoking the leaves was to soothe coughs and was recommended by Dioscórides, Galen and Pliny; to relieve asthma and the difficult breathing associated with chronic bronchitis. How times change.

Recently there has been some concern about the presence of pyrrolizidine alkaloids in the leaves which may have an adverse effect on the liver.

Elecampane
Inula helenium

Introduced by the Romans, this is a very distinctive plant – the flower head is reminiscent of a sunflower and the leaves are large and pale green but it's the root that is used medicinally. Many years ago sections of root were boiled in sugar to produce 'cough candy'. The root should be harvested in the autumn.

The root is very aromatic; the volatile oils can diffuse from the digestive tract into the lungs where it has an expectorant effect – enabling the lungs to release phlegm by coughing. Also soothing and anti-microbial. Another important herb for treating lung conditions.

Lobelia
Lobelia inflata

This variety of lobelia has white flowers and large seed pods hence its name. The herb is gathered after flowering when the seed pods have developed.

A Class 20 herb, it should only be used by a qualified herbalist.

Another name for lobelia is puke weed as this is what happens if you take too much of this herb. Samuel Thompson, an 18th century American herbalist, had his first experience of prescribing herbs when as a teenager he encouraged an unwell farm worker to eat some lobelia – the man threw up and felt much better. Samuel had decided on his future career. He was ultimately responsible via Dr. Isah Coffin (a prodigy of Samuel's) for reintroducing herbal medicine into England during the industrial revolution.

Lobelia, when taken in the correct dose, has a relaxing effect. I use it in mixtures to treat lung conditions; when the lungs and surrounding tissue are relaxed it makes it easier to breathe. Particularly useful in treating asthma and bronchitis.

It's also included in my joint and muscle cream – relaxed tissue absorbs the other herbs more easily.

Mullein
Verbascum thapsus

A beautiful, majestic plant with large furry leaves and a tall spike of yellow flowers, it can be found in the wild throughout Europe and Asia. When I find it locally it's usually because it's escaped from someone's garden. If you pick the flowers and put them in a clear glass jar with some organic sunflower oil, and place the jar in a sunny position for a few weeks you end up with a bright yellow oil which soothes irritated and inflamed skin.

The leaves produce a remedy which is soothing for irritated and dry coughs, specifically bronchitis.

This herb is bi-annual – the first year a rosette of leaves are produced – these leaves make an excellent lung tonic. The second year the spike of yellow flowers develops.

Wild Cherry Bark
Prunus serontina

The inner bark is used – this is harvested in autumn or spring when it is easier to remove the bark.

Wild cherry bark soothes the cough reflex which makes it invaluable for irritating, dry coughs. It shouldn't be used when the cough is productive because it's important for the phlegm and mucus to be coughed up, otherwise the lungs might become infected and develop a more serious condition.

Kidney herbs

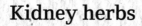

Pot Marigold Flowers
Calendula officinalis

Marigold has brightly coloured yellow or orange flowers which are sticky due to the resin present in them.

Calendula is a favourite herb of mine because it does so much:

It's a key ingredient in a kidney tea mixture that I make – *calendula* is anti-inflammatory, anti-bacterial, anti-viral and anti-fungal. I also use *calendula* flowers on their own as a tea for people who are suffering from the yeast overgrowth known as candida because of this anti-fungal property.

Calendula heals tissues, both inside and outside the body. Early on in my practice I was told that you should make sure that cuts and abrasions are cleaned thoroughly, not only to avoid infection but also to prevent any dirt being healed into the wound particularly if *calendula* ointment was being applied to the area.

Lichen sclerosis is a very unpleasant itchy condition which affects the skin anywhere on the body, sometimes on the scalp, in the mouth and occasionally around the vagina/penis – very itchy, shiny purple patches develop which can become thickened and keratinised.

A patient developed this condition around her vagina – the usual treatment is steroid cream which has the side effect of thinning skin. She asked if there was anything herbal that she could try and I suggested using *calendula* ointment. She has found this very helpful – relieving the itching and healing the affected patches. There is research which shows that this condition responds well to supplementation with Beta Carotene – *calendula* is very high in Beta Carotene which contributes to the vibrant orange/yellow colour of its flowers.

Golden Rod
Solidago virgaurea

Golden rod is a relatively tall plant with yellow flower heads.

I have begun to use this herb more than I used to; it is very soothing, anti-bacterial and it dissolves kidney stones. It is a key ingredient in my kidney tea mixture – I prescribe this as a preventative for cystitis and also to help people recover from cystitis. Cystitis is often due to an E-coli infection in the bladder usually affecting women, the main symptoms being 'like peeing broken glass' and needing to urinate frequently; occasionally blood is present and a high temperature. This condition needs treating quickly and effectively because if left untreated the infection can travel up the uretras into the kidneys, which becomes a much more serious condition and can cause kidney damage.

Apart from drinking the kidney tea formula, drink lots of water to flush out the bladder. Half a teaspoon of bicarbonate of soda in a little water with a squeeze of lemon juice is excellent at easing the discomfort. E-coli enjoy an acidic environment and bicarbonate of soda is very alkaline. If the symptoms haven't resolved or at least eased within 24 hours go to your GP with a urine sample.

I use golden rod's ability to dissolve kidney stones for anyone who has had kidney stones, along with other appropriate herbs to help prevent them forming again.

Golden rod is a useful mucous membrane tonic which benefits the urinary tract and can help reduce upper respiratory catarrh.

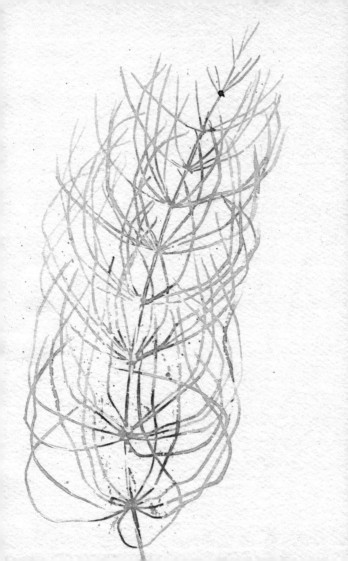

Horsetail
Equisetum arvense

Horsetail is an ancient herb; it looks like a very small and spindly fir tree, and it grows in damp ground – once it's in your garden there is no known way to get rid of it.

When you pick horsetail it feels very dry, and if you scrunch it up it can feel dry and gritty. Years ago when pewter was popular this herb was used to clean it – horsetail contains silica which creates an abrasive cleaner making pewter shine like silver.

The silica in horsetail is valuable for healing 'transitional' tissue – tissue that stretches – particularly the lungs and bladder.

It also reduces bleeding – I include this herb in my cystitis mix because there may be some bleeding present but also because it encourages the bladder to remain elastic after the infection. This tea, which also contains marigolds, golden rod and an antimicrobial herb called buchu, is recommended for people who have a tendency towards developing cystitis and it can often prevent the infection developing. This is not a treatment for acute cystitis.

This herb also goes into many chest and lung mixtures for a similar reason – it helps the lungs remain elastic and deep breathing is a good defence against developing lung infections.

Wild Bergamot
Monarda fistulosa

A fragrant plant with a beautiful pale purple flower,
I came across this plant through reading Matthew
Wood's 'Herbal Wisdom' book, where he talked about
its cooling properties – useful for burns and cystitis –
in such a persuasive way that I bought some seeds
and grew some plants.

Although Matthew talks about using three or four
drops at a time, I have found that 10 to 20 drops makes
it most effective for my patients. It is excellent for
soothing the pain of cystitis – just like it says in
Matthew's book.

A few years ago, I had a patient who had suffered
brain damage as a consequence of contracting Q fever.
One of her symptoms was vertigo – *Monarda fistulosa*
helped reduce the severity of this symptom
significantly.

I especially like studying and working with herbs
that have beneficial effects on apparently wildly
different symptoms or conditions, such as in this case.

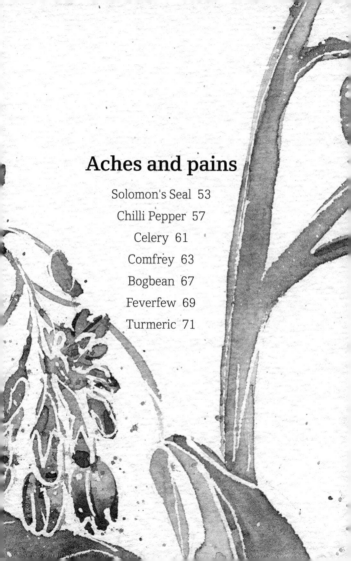

Aches and pains

Solomon's Seal
Polygonatum multiflorum

An early spring plant that grows in damp shady places, it has large leaves and a double string of bell–like white flowers.

I have only been using Solomon's seal – the root in particular – for the last six-seven years. I again came across it in Matthew Wood's 'Herbal Wisdom' book – not only did its properties sound amazing, I also had a large patch of it growing in the garden. Shortly after finding the herb in my garden I went to an American herbal conference where I discovered that many US herbalists used it to great effect.

While I was travelling around New York State (1000 miles in 10 days) an old injury from falling on my coccyx whilst showing my children how to slide on a frozen tarn 15 years previously – how we laughed – began to become very painful. All the sitting and driving had aggravated it. One of our visits was to a herb farm. During breakfast one morning I found myself talking about the pain in my coccyx – in no time I was provided with Solomon's seal tincture to drink and receiving a Zero Balancing treatment. I haven't had any pain or discomfort since.

The herbalists on the farm told us a story about a neighbour's dog who had been hit by a car, dislocating the dog's jaw – the neighbour called in to the farm on the way to see the vet to ask if someone could cradle the dog during the 30 minute journey. A young lad volunteered to help but first grabbed a handful of Solomon's seal root and held it against the dog's head and jaw – they returned 15 minutes later because the dogs jaw had realigned and there was no need to go to the vet.

That's what Solomon's seal does – it realigns bones, tissues and flesh – I now use it a lot in my practice and its effectiveness never fails to amaze me.

Chilli Pepper
Capsicum minimum

A very spicy herb; it is a member of the Solanaceae family which also includes potatoes, sweet peppers and tomatoes.

I use this herb in tiny amounts, unsurprisingly, almost exclusively in sinus mixtures to thin mucus and encourage the nose to run and therefore unblock congested sinuses (I'm sure many of you will have noticed this effect after eating a hot curry). Sinuses are very narrow bony tubes that drain the eyes, nose and throat. If they become congested, swelling and inflammation around the eyes and cheeks can develop, which is very painful.

Capsicum can also be used externally – I use it in my joint and muscle cream to heat the affected area and increase the blood supply – this combination allows the other herbs to be absorbed more efficiently and for toxins to be carried away from the area. It should only be used on 'cold' stiff and painful areas. If it is a recent injury and the area is hot apply frozen peas or similar.

Many years ago, before I realised that I shouldn't provide herbal information over the phone (being sued for this sort of thing going wrong was in its infancy),

I was phoned by a woman whose husband was in tremendous pain with a shingles rash. *Capsicum* contains a chemical called substance P which has pain relieving properties – I suggested that she obtain an ointment called 'Fiery Jack' (its main ingredient is *capsicum*) and apply it to her husband's rash. I didn't think any more about it but a couple of weeks later I received a card from her thanking me for my advice – her husband had benefitted from the *capsicum* ointment treatment tremendously.

I do not recommend that you try this at home as some people can be sensitive to 'Fiery Jack' and its ilk.

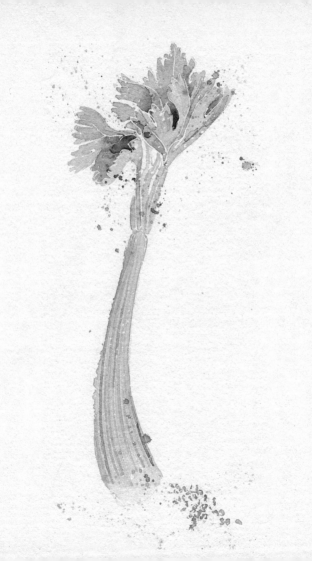

Celery
Apium graveolens

A very familiar vegetable, recently it has been
suggested that it can cure pretty much any ailment you
care to mention. I like this herb/vegetable a lot but I
wouldn't make quite such impressive claims about its
healing properties. The tincture is made from the seeds;
I use the vegetable in my juices.

The main problem with celery is that some people
really dislike its distinctive taste.

I tend to use it in the form of a tincture to treat gout
as it has the ability to dissolve uric acid crystals which
can form in small joints causing great pain. It's also a
diuretic which encourages the kidneys to flush uric
acid out of the body.

I use it in my green juices if I'm feeling achy or stiff
– the results are almost immediate.

Comfrey
Symphytum officinale

The leaves are the part that is used these days –
in the old days people used to use the root as well.
However, due to the presence of pyrrolizidine alkaloids
the root is no longer used and the use of the leaves is
under consideration. This herb grows in large clumps
by the side of roads and in damp areas. The leaves are
large and bristly, the flowers range in colour from pale
to deep purple even on the same plant.

As a herbal student I made comfrey leaf fritters –
the leaves dipped in batter and fried – delicious, melt
in the mouth food and not a bristle in sight.

The leaves are often fermented in rainwater to
produce a nutritious feed for hungry plants like
tomatoes.

The country name for this herb is 'knit bone' and
that's what it does by speeding up the healing of bones,
tendons and ligaments as well as skin. The chemical
allantoin is considered to be responsible for this plant's
remarkable healing properties which encourages tissue
healing.

I use this as a cream, ointment or oil to apply
externally on just about any damaged tissue except

open wounds. When taken as a tea it not only heals but has the ability to reduce pain as well.

I have a patient with severe osteoporosis and I recommended comfrey tea to try to strengthen her bones and stabilise the osteoporosis. It was only when she told me that she had managed to come off all her painkillers that I realised how useful comfrey is in painful conditions as well. I have encouraged other patients to use comfrey tea for pain relief with equally impressive effects.

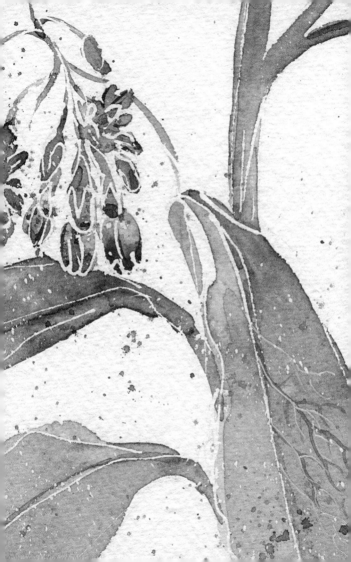

Bogbean
Menyanthes trifoliata

This herb grows in bogs or shallow ponds, has three medium sized leaves and a short spike of white flowers tinged with pink.

The part used is the leaves – I use them as a tincture in mixtures to treat rheumatic conditions. This herb has a stimulating effect on the digestive system relieving mild constipation and stimulates the flow of bile – improving the digestion of fats. If we don't have regular bowel movements – regular means daily – toxins are reabsorbed after such extended periods and this can cause inflammation of the joints among other health problems. I once asked this question of a patient without specifying what I meant by regular and she replied – yes, every week! – some people are pleased to only have a bowel movement twice a month.

Feverfew
Tanacetum parthenium

A member of the daisy family – the flowers look very much like common daisies but with more petals, the leaves are vigorous and the whole plant grows to about eight inches in height. When a leaf is picked a distinctive smell is released. It has a very bitter taste.

It is correctly known for its pain relieving properties, originally used through the centuries as a treatment for migraines – particularly those that are eased by heat. Some of the folk traditions I've heard have said that the best way to take it is one leaf eaten between two slices of bread – but as some people can have a dramatic allergic reaction to the leaf a proper level of caution is encouraged.

I use it as a tincture for the treatment of migraines and to reduce the pain of arthritis. A trial to test the effectiveness of feverfew in the treatment of migraines found that people who had migraines and arthritis noticed that both improved when taking feverfew. It is believed that it interrupts the prostaglandin pathway – a pain pathway – by doing so it reduces the perception of pain.

Turmeric
Curcuma longa

A relative of ginger, it is also the root that is used
– the root is much smaller than ginger and is bright
yellow or orange.

Turmeric is a new and exciting superfood whose
properties have been known throughout India for
thousands of years.

It is a powerful anti-inflammatory, thins bile
(improving the digestion of fats) and is a useful anti-
oxidant. It also helps with lowering cholesterol.

I use it in mixtures for people who are suffering
from pain, inflammation and gall stones.

A few years ago I had a patient who had an
inherited condition which caused high temperatures
which was beginning to affect her kidneys. An unusual
condition that hadn't had much research into finding
a treatment – a trial treatment was available but there
were significant side effects. I prescribed turmeric and
her episodes of fever were much reduced. The tincture
has a distinctive taste and so she chose to take her
turmeric in capsule form.

Digestion

Ginger
Zingiber officinale

The root of ginger is the part used for cooking and used medicinally. The flowers are spikes of red and orange – very dramatic and they have a mild ginger scent.

The root can be used fresh or dried as a powder – when added to boiling water this drink is excellent for treating colds and flu by helping you to 'sweat it out' and also for treating nausea – morning sickness, sea sickness, travel sickness etc.

I also add the tincture to mixtures to help warm up and soothe digestion.

Agrimony
Agrimonia eupatoria

A small spike of yellow flowers which turn into sticky burrs – this is agrimony; the leaves and flowers are used but not the burrs.

It's a gentle astringent and tonic which can be used to support the digestive system. I use it particularly when there is gastric reflux – when the sphincter at the top of the stomach allows some stomach contents to travel upwards causing burning of the oesophagus and throat. Agrimony seems to be able to strengthen this valve and its bitter element acts as a tonic to the digestive system making it work more efficiently.

I have also found that small amounts of agrimony tincture have a calming effect on the nervous system.

Hops
Humulus lupulus

A climbing herb which grows many metres in a season, it has flowers or strobiles hanging in clumps along the bines.

Hops have a soporific quality – they can make you sleepy. They also have a desensitising effect on the gut.

Heine Zeylstra taught us that 'hops may make even mild depression much worse.' During a seminar for herbalists on depression, Desmond Corrigan – Associate Professor at The School of Pharmacy and Pharmaceutical Sciences at Trinity College Dublin – was puzzled that his audience didn't use hops medicinally as much as he expected. He explained that he hadn't found that they exacerbated depression. From that day forward I have found hops to be invaluable; they are in the sleep mix I have been making for years and they also form a major part of any IBS (irritable bowel syndrome) mix that I prescribe. The hops have a local anaesthetic effect on the bowel which reduces the 'irritability' of the gut. Some people may take from this that beer drinkers do not suffer from irritable bowel syndrome – this is sadly not the case. There are other herbs that are equally important and are included in any IBS blend that I make up. Each mixture is prepared specifically for the patient.

Meadowsweet
Filipendula ulmaria

Meadowsweet contains salicyns which give it pain relieving properties; these are very mild but even so this herb can be used to help ease discomfort and stomach aches. It has a variety of uses but I use it in digestive mixtures because it balances the amount of acid the stomach produces.

Too little acid being produced means that food stays in the stomach for a long time before proteins are broken down into amino acids by pepsin. This can cause pain and discomfort because the protective mucous coating which covers the lining of the stomach may break down, allowing the acid and enzymes present to corrode the stomach lining, or the cardiac sphincter at the top of the stomach may weaken due to the presence of hydrochloric acid as may the sphincter at the bottom of the stomach. Stomach contents leaving the stomach the wrong way (up) or too soon (down) means that an acidic solution will come into contact with unprotected epithelial tissue and cause pain or a burning sensation.

The alternative situation is that there is too much acid present for the amount of food/protein that needs breaking down and it burns through the protective

mucous coating again causing a burning sensation
– often painful.

Meadowsweet balances the levels of acid and
protects the stomach, particularly soothing gastric
hyperacidity and ulcers. It also encourages tissue repair
and is gently astringent.

I use it in digestive mixtures with marshmallow root
– a root that produces a thick mucilaginous tincture or
decoction which coats and soothes the digestive tract.

Marshmallow
Althea officinalis

Marshmallow grows in damp areas and has purple flowers. The root and leaves are used; the root is particularly mucilaginous.

I use this herb to soothe an inflamed digestive tract. If gastric reflux occurs, stomach contents moving up into the unprotected oesophagus cause a burning sensation – it's very hard to ease the discomfort of this burning sensation. A glass of water doesn't even touch the discomfort but marshmallow root does. It coats the area with a protective film which soothes and protects the area. If gastric reflux happens frequently it can cause scarring of the oesophagus which may in time become cancerous. Reflux is not a condition to ignore. Although many people treat it with antacids and other over the counter treatments, getting to the underlying cause is the best long-term treatment. Sometimes this is stress and anxiety, and sometimes it's due to a congested gallbladder or other digestive problem.

Mint
Mentha piperita

Peppermint is a very fast acting herb; I use the top leaves and only before flowering. It has a distinctive smell.

This herb is mainly used to aid digestion; it's no accident that most indigestion treatments are mint flavoured. Mint stimulates the gallbladder to produce bile, bile is needed to emulsify fats and break them down into fatty acids. If you don't produce enough bile the breakdown of fat happens very slowly which can make you feel very uncomfortable and can cause indigestion.

Mint also has anti-spasmodic properties – the griping sensation than can happen during a bout of IBS (irritable bowel syndrome) or gastroenteritis can be eased almost instantly by taking a capsule of mint essential oil (available at all good herbal and health food shops).

Mint has the ability to stimulate temperature receptors; many of you will have noticed water tastes extra cold after eating a mint, this is caused by menthol (the main essential oil in mint).

Barberry
Berberis vulgaris

The root and outer bark of branches are used – they have a strong yellow colour.

This herb has a tonic effect on the liver, gall bladder, pancreas and spleen. I use it as a tincture when there is a problem with digestion, especially difficulty digesting fats which is a distinguishing factor. It has an anti-inflammatory effect on the gall bladder and is a gentle laxative. I like the fact that *Berberis vulgaris* is also a tonic for the spleen – the spleen is often overlooked when it comes to tonics.

The berberine found in *berberis* and hydrastis/golden seal has a powerful anti-bacterial effect, especially on the digestive system which is useful in cases of food poisoning.

Cardamom
Eletteria cardamomum

Fragrant seeds that grow in warmer climates, these
seeds are from several species of the *eletteria* family
with *Eleteria cardamomum* being known as 'true'
cardamom.

I use this tincture as a warming digestive herb –
it gently improves a sluggish digestion and helps to
dissipate wind. Gasses generated by fermentation
can be a side effect of a slow digestion and this can
be embarrassing.

I also use cardamom with laxative herbs as these
can cause 'griping' which is unpleasant and painful
but cardamom prevents this from happening.

Coriander
Coriandrum sativum

Its leaves have a very distinctive smell and are used a lot in Asian cooking; the flowers are a mass of tiny white blooms.

The seeds are also used in cooking and as a tea or tincture.

As a member of the umbeliferae family, it is helpful in relieving trapped wind or spasms within the digestive system (all members of the family have this effect to a greater or lesser extent). Also useful in combination with spirulena in removing heavy metals from the body. This is a mixture that should be taken alongside vitamin C when having amalgam fillings removed.

Wormwood
Artemisia absinthium

A very fragrant plant, it has a distinctive bitter quality. It grows as a shrub or bush and has many relatives who also contain volatile oils. Southernwood has a lemony fragrance and was used dried to keep moths away from clothes. Sweet Annie is used in the treatment of malaria, and other parasites and infective agents. Mugwort is used in Chinese medicine as moxa, a treatment often used alongside acupuncture.

When I was doing my herbal training, one herbalist I spent time with often added wormwood to mixtures to potentiate the other herbs in a mixture; to make everything work together more effectively. It strengthens weak digestive systems.

It is less medicinal when infused alongside anise and fennel among other herbs for the production of absinthe, a notoriously strong alcoholic drink which gained renown for its potency and hallucinogenic effects in 19th century France. Modern investigation indicates that the psychoactive nature of 'the green fairy' may have been overstated but the stories remain. Another effect on absinthe drinkers was a form of epilepsy due to the presence of thujone in the herb which is toxic to the brain.

Wormwood, as the name suggests, has been used for millennia for treating infestations of parasites – particularly intestinal worms.

Walnut
Juglans nigra

Walnuts grow on trees – you can identify these by the presence of walnuts – these trees have a pale bark and reddish elongated leaves.

Green walnuts are an excellent digestive tonic – as they support the liver, have a laxative effect and help clear skin problems, particularly scrofula conditions and eczema. They are also used as a vermifuge – worm killer.

The dark brown colour that is produced by walnuts when they are processed in any way is thought to contain iodine – this makes it a useful herb for supporting people with an underactive thyroid. The thyroid is a gland which is butterfly shaped and is found in the throat area. This gland is responsible for regulating our metabolism – an underactive thyroid causes a lack of energy, feeling cold, poor memory, thinning hair and constipation, to name but a few symptoms.

I have used this herb a number of times in mixtures to support people who have a suggestion of an underactive thyroid and it's been very effective.

Immune system

Echinacea
Echinacea purpurea

A pink flowered daisy-looking plant but much bigger at 18" to 2ft in height. The root is the part used although a milder effect can be gained from the flowers (the root particularly but also the flowers cause a slight tingling sensation in the mouth when the tea or tincture is drunk – this is considered to be a sign of its potency).

This herb is native to North America and is not found in the wild here in the UK. Do not despair though, many people grow it in their gardens as a species of rubekia.

Echinacea has a very well founded reputation for boosting the immune system as an anti-viral, often helping to protect people from infections or speeding up the healing process. Much of the research carried out on the efficacy of echinacea has been focussed on the root of echinacea purpurea which has been shown to be effective in treating viral infections of the upper respiratory system – ideal for supporting people who have had the coronavirus.

I must have taken gallons of echinacea tincture over the years but I was never convinced that it was as effective as I was led to believe. Eventually I decided to combine it with some other herbs; currently elderberry and astragalus – this is a mixture that I find boosts my immune system impressively. Having talked to many herbalists I now realise that echinacea is very effective, but for some people it needs to be mixed with additional herbs to get the full benefit. This has allowed me to cut down on my tincture consumption – with some relief!

Elderberry | Elderflower
Sambucus nigra

This is an amazing shrub or if left long enough a small tree. The flowers are a sure sign that spring has sprung – a mass of yellowy white flowers with an amazing fragrance – which can cause sneezing, especially in those who suffer from hay fever.

Elderflower tea or cordial are delicious drinks with the added advantage that they dry up runny eyes and noses – symptoms associated with hay fever. Elderflower tea is also helpful in relieving lung congestion, especially in children. The reduction of mucus is helpful in easing all these conditions.

Elderflower tincture is a key ingredient in the sinus drops that I make to relieve sinus congestion. This mixture contains an equal quantity of chamomile tincture with a selection of warming herbs.

Elderberries have a long and well deserved reputation as having a powerful anti-viral effect – see above. The leaves have emetic properties ie. make you sick. The bark has a purgative effect ie. the total emptying of the bowel.

Neither of these last two parts of the elder tree are used in my tinctures these days; they are far too dramatic for my taste and that of my patients.

Garlic
Alium sativum

Garlic is very familiar to just about everyone because of its distinctive taste and smell. The wild garlic that grows here in the UK doesn't have a bulb but the leaves make up for it with their pungent scent.

Garlic is a very powerful anti-microbial. During the First World War it was used to keep wounds infection-free similar to the way we use antibiotics now. When I was travelling with a friend around Asia she developed what I now know to be a tropical ulcer on her ankle. I hadn't started training as a herbalist but I did have a few notes with me; packing the ulcer with garlic caused great pain but no infection, another lesson learnt (yes, we are still friends – I apologised a lot).

Garlic is also a useful anti-fungal and has anti-viral actions as well as being effective against parasites. It lowers blood pressure, thins the blood and lowers cholesterol. Garlic also helps to encourage the growth of good bacteria in the digestive tract in the form of a prebiotic.

When I was training to be a herbalist I used to eat a lot of garlic – everyone did. One day I chopped up the garlic as usual and swallowed it on an empty stomach –

the pain was intense and I learned from this to only eat raw garlic as part of a meal or after a meal.

When I travel to far off places, I always take a bulb of garlic with me and have a clove of garlic on toast every morning – this helps to protect me from digestive upsets and fascinates the uninitiated.

Skin

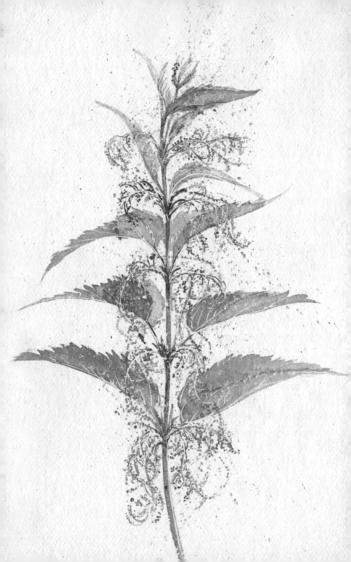

Nettles
Urtica dioica

The top leaves before flowering are the part to use.
If you're not sure that you have the correct plant its
sting will give it away.

It is easy to underestimate the humble nettle
especially if there is a large patch of them in your
garden somewhere where you would like to grow
something else. Even in an early Saxon herbal –
'The Leechbook of Bald' – a comment is made about
eliminating nettles being very hard work and in this
case nothing has changed for at least 1000 years.

Nettles are nature's vitamin and mineral supplement;
they only grow in areas where the soil is very
nutritious – compost heaps for example. They are very
good at absorbing nutrients from the soil. The sting is
generated from an injection of formic acid from the
hairs on the leaves and on the stem; formic acid is also
found in stinging ants. If you brush against a nettle you
will be stung but if you grip a leaf firmly it won't sting
you. There is an amount of practice to this that many
may find daunting so I recommend gloves when
handling fresh nettles.

When I was younger my grandfather used to tell me

stories about his childhood; as he was born in 1896 his stories were from a very different world. One story that he told me was about a family that lived close by, just outside Manchester – they were so poor that they had to eat nettles. We would sit together marvelling at such poverty and concerned that they would be badly stung as they ate their nettles.

Fast forward, sadly my grandfather has died but I now know that boiled nettle tops and especially nettle soup is a very nutritious meal. To prove this to my children I made large pans of this soup when they were young and on one memorable occasion when they had friends round to play, I placed steaming bowls of soup in front of each child and then went to do something important. After a while I thought that they were being unnaturally quiet and I put my head around the door to see a table with steaming bowls of nettle soup but no children – the soup had made the children disappear. They all turned up later however, none the worse for their experience when chocolate biscuits were being released from the packet.

I use nettle tea and tincture to soothe itchy skin conditions – the physio medicalists who evolved from the botanical medicalists in the late 1800s used to call the effect that nettles have as 'blood cleansing'. They certainly have a tonic effect which is very useful and effective.

Nettle roots contain a chemical that is similar to testosterone – the prostate gland enlarges when levels of testosterone drop in an effort to make use of all available testosterone. By using nettle root the prostate doesn't need to grow, because there are sufficient available testosterone–like chemicals to fill the receptor sites on the prostate.

Nettle seeds have a reputation as a diuretic – enabling the body to release excess fluids – and I have used them successfully a number of times. Although my current diuretic of choice is dandelion leaves as they contain high levels of potassium; an element which is often lost when diuretics are used.

Goose Grass
Clivers | Galium aparine

Another gardeners' favourite – this herb climbs across gardens, over walls and other plants. The tiny hooks on its stem allow it to climb and attach to anything including animals' fur and people's clothes.

This spring herb, along with nettle tops, black currant leaves and dandelion leaves, was included in an old Cumbrian delicacy called Easter Ledge pudding, also known as *polygonum bistort* – a celebration of young green spring herbs which were boiled up with barley. Easter Ledges flourish around Easter time when Easter Ledge pudding was made to celebrate the beginning of spring and the end of winter.

Galium aparine is also a diuretic but it works more on the lymphatic system – draining enlarged lymph nodes in the arm pit, breast and neck. Recently a patient with a swollen hand has been drinking *galium* tea which has helped reduce the swelling while she waits for further investigations into the underlying cause.

It is also a very cooling herb which I include in mixtures for 'hot' skin conditions.

Chickweed
Stellaria media

In spring chickweed grows vigorously especially in damp areas – in farm gateways for example. This plant produces copious amounts of slimy sap; it has even been known to cause tractor tyres to spin.

This sap or juice is also very soothing and cooling – I prescribe chickweed cream to people with itchy skin conditions – particularly children. It doesn't heal but the soothing effect allows the body to heal itself.

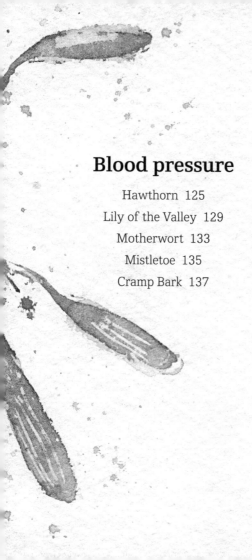

Blood pressure

Hawthorn
Crataegus oxyacanthoides

Known as May flower, hawthorn flowers in May producing beautiful white/pinky flowers; the berries form around September.

Hawthorn increases the circulation to the heart muscle itself via the coronary circulation. This gives the heart additional support and allows more oxygenated blood to get to the body.

I use this herb a lot – possibly more than any other herb – so anyone with high blood pressure will have this herb in their mixture.

I have had a number of patients with heart problems, all of whom have benefitted from taking hawthorn tincture. One patient from some years ago was a man who had an episode of bacterial endocarditis 30 years previously – an infection affecting the heart valves – he found that by taking hawthorn his heart worked more efficiently and he had more energy.

Another patient had a heart attack in her 40s found it difficult to tolerate the medication prescribed – I made up three tonics for her:

1. Mainly hawthorn with some Indian myrrh –

traditionally used to reduce any arterio sclerotic plaques present.

2. A selection of herbs to ensure that her blood pressure remained within the normal range.

3. Heart drops – lily of the valley and motherwort – to use if there was any suggestion of angina. If angina developed then she would use her GTN (glyceryl trinitrate) spray.

This patient has been taking these herbs or similar for five years with very few episodes of angina. She was asked to go to Manchester for genetic testing because she had had a heart attack at such a young age. After sitting in the waiting room for a while she was invited into the consulting room where numerous tests were carried out on her heart, eventually they asked her why she had come to the clinic because her heart was in excellent shape. She explained about the genetic testing and she was told to go to the clinic around the corner – where the testing was carried out – she had spent most of the day in the wrong clinic. The side effect of this was that she was reassured about her heart health and put it down to the herbs because she wasn't taking any other medication.

Lily of the Valley
Convallaria majis

A spring flower, they are tiny, fragrant bell-like flowers with spear-shaped leaves – a smaller version of Solomon's seal.

This herb is a Class 20 herb which means that it can only be prescribed by a qualified Medical Herbalist.

It has the effect of slowing the heart down – if the heart is struggling for any reason including heart failure – which means that each time the heart beats blood goes backwards as well as forwards through a weakened valve in the heart – this can be compensated for by the body speeding up the heart rate. This is unsustainable for any length of time because the blood flow becomes less efficient the faster the heart beats.

Lily of the valley not only slows the heart down but also encourages the heart to beat more strongly. This effect ensures that the blood circulates more efficiently around the body and creates less stress overall.

The first time I prescribed this herb was for an elderly woman who had woken up in the middle of the night with a tremendous pressure on her chest. Right heart failure will cause a backlog of blood in the lungs and liquid will diffuse into the surrounding tissue causing the sensation of pressure. This was the diagnosis that she was given but she was reluctant to take medication from the doctor – ultimately it was agreed with her GP that she would take a diuretic from the GP and herbs from me. The main treatment that I prescribed was lily of the valley drops with hawthorn (heart tonic) and dandelion leaf (diuretic and potassium).

She didn't have another episode again, and lived independently looking after her house and garden until her death years later at the age of 94.

The first recorded trial on the use, efficacy, and safety of a herb was carried out by Derbyshire doctor William Withering in 1785 using turkeys. As a new doctor to the area he noticed that people would treat oedema/fluid retention by eating foxglove leaves, but he also noticed that sometimes people who treated themselves in this way died suddenly. He wondered if this had anything to do with the quantity of leaf or root that they had eaten. He separated his turkeys into groups and fed them different amounts of foxglove leaves, roots, and flowers – some had no ill effect and some died, and some died after appearing well when their dose of foxglove was increased; thereby proving the importance of giving the correct form and dose of the foxglove to his patients.

Foxgloves have a similar effect to lily of the valley on the heart – slowing it down and making it beat more strongly/effectively but the difference is that the foxglove leaves have a very small 'therapeutic window' i.e. it's very easy to overdose the patient causing their heart to stop. Herbalists no longer use foxgloves therapeutically but an extract is used in mainstream medicine in the form of digoxin.

Motherwort
Leonurus cardiaca

This herb is dark green and the seeds are spiky; it grows to around 18″ height.

Motherwort has a close affinity to both the heart and the uterus; which in Chinese medicine is an obvious link – less so for us in the west.

Motherwort has a gentle stimulating effect on the uterus; it is helpful in bringing on a delayed period, or historically for ensuring the release of the afterbirth when a baby has been born. Definitely not a herb to use during pregnancy.

This herb's effect on the heart is relaxing and soothing, easing pressure or tension in the chest.

I use it in combination with lily of the valley to treat angina – the dose has to be very precise due to the possibility of slowing the heart down too much. It is very effective and works quickly but if the symptoms aren't relieved by these herbs, using a GTN spray (*Gyceryl Trinitrate*) is the next necessary step. This treatment should only be used under the supervision of a Medical Herbalist.

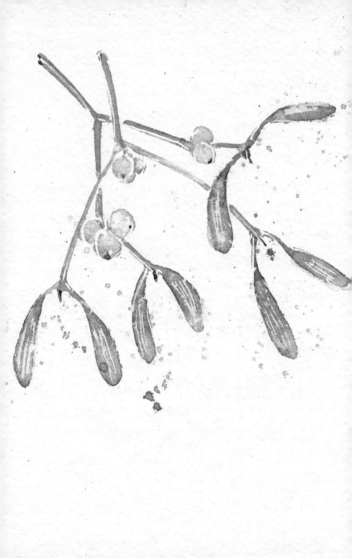

Mistletoe
Viscum album

As seen at Christmas with its green twigs and translucent berries, this herb is a parasite which mainly grows on apple, poplar, or oak trees.

Only dried twigs of mistletoe are used, not the berries as they are poisonous.

The tea or tincture has the effect of soothing the heart and the nervous system – it acts on the vagus nerve reducing the speed of the heart and strengthening the capillaries, making the circulation more efficient and thereby reducing blood pressure.

This is a herb I use a lot in mixtures to reduce blood pressure.

Cramp Bark
Viburnum opulus

A small bush or shrub, it has masses of white flowers which have larger petals on the outside and smaller ones towards the centre. From a distance they look a little like hydrangea flowers.

The bark is harvested in late spring and dried before using as a tea or tincture. This bark has a distinctive smell which develops over time – the aroma is created by the oxidation of valerianic acid. This constituent is also found in the herb valerian.

Its name gives its use – it relaxes muscle cramps. A few years ago I was asked to make up a cream that a massage therapist wanted to use on a mutual client with cerebral palsy to relieve muscle spasms. I made up a cream containing cramp bark and added some lavender essential oil to take the edge off the smell and a small amount of lobelia to relax the tissues – the report back was that it had made our patient more comfortable, not stopping the muscle spasms but making them less intense and painful.

Relaxing tense muscles also helps lower blood pressure, because it allows arteries to expand more easily thereby reducing the pressure within the circulatory system.

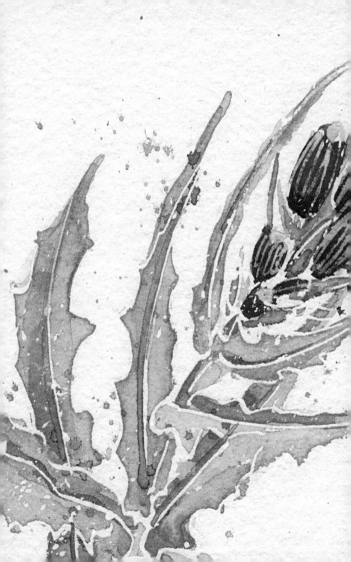

Soperifics

Valerian
Valeriana officinalis

A spring flower that looks a lot like cow parsley – many tiny white flowers tinged with pink making up a flower head that appears on road sides and in gardens with a distinctive scent. A flower arranger friend of mine gathered some herbs from the garden and made a beautiful arrangement which was in the house for several days before we worked out that the unusual smell wasn't a visiting tomcat, it was in fact coming from the valerian flowers in the arrangement.

People love or hate the smell – in a tincture the aroma has a sort of fruity smell but the dried herb smells like old unwashed socks – cats love it. Once, several years ago, I came home to the sight of our cat lying in the middle of a heap of dried valerian root – it had chewed through a cardboard box and several bags to get to it but it was very happy if a little spaced out.

In the days when NHS GPs had to attend study days, I was invited to speak at several complementary health days. The first time – when I wasn't quite sure what to expect – I took along plenty of herb samples to hand round. When I uncorked the valerian bottle the room filled with the smell very quickly and immediately a member of the audience jumped up, ordered me to put the top back on the bottle and then quickly left the room. Confused, I carried on, finished my talk, answered questions and sat down to listen to the next talk. The next speaker was a homeopath who looked familiar – he was the man who had found valerian so offensive. During the lunch break several GPs asked me the name of the herb that got rid of homeopaths – I certainly learned a lot during those study days.

Valerian is very calming – known as a herbal tranquiliser – yet it doesn't cause tiredness. It's in my sleep mix because of its calming qualities and because it improves the quality of sleep. It is a particularly fast acting herb and you only need a few drops in water to benefit from its effect. I find it to be excellent for exams, interviews and tests.

From time to time it can have the opposite effect. Some people find valerian stimulating and not calming at all. My friend's small son found the valerian drops and by the time she found him he was on the ceiling! Keep medicines and herbs out of reach of children.

Passion Flower
Passiflora incarnata

A climbing plant that has beautiful and often intensely coloured flowers. This is not a herb that you will see on a herb walk in Cumbria in the wild but it grows well in sheltered spots in gardens.

The dried leaves are used rather than the distinctively delicate looking flowers.

There are over 500 recognised species of passion flower; *passiflora incarnata* or purple passion flower being the most widely cultivated.

This is a calming herb which is also anti-spasmodic and eases pain – I have used it to help patients suffering from Parkinson's to feel more comfortable. Due to its effect of enabling people to 'ease into sleep' it is a key ingredient of my sleep mixture.

Lime Flower
Tilia europaea

The flowers are tiny but, with a surprisingly strong perfume, make a pleasantly fragrant tea and a syrupy tincture.

Relaxing and calming, this is a very relaxing bedtime drink or a tea which soothes anxiety.

Lime flowers have the reputation of protecting against developing arteriosclerosis and their relaxing element can be useful in lowering blood pressure.

Californian Poppy
Eschscholzia californica

There are many members of the poppy family and they all to a greater or lesser extent promote sleep and ease pain.

In the South Lakes we have an abundance of Welsh poppies which are all yellow, Californian poppies are a similar size and shape but the flowers are different shades of orange and the leaves are much finer.

The flowers and leaves are used.

Although not in the same league as the opium poppy, this poppy also encourages sleep – it seems to enable people with busy minds to switch off and go to sleep. Most importantly it's not addictive, at least not at the levels I use. It has a reputation for easing the pain of gallbladder colic.

Wild Lettuce
Lactuca virosa

This doesn't look like the lettuce that goes into our salads; it has very small leaves which grow into a spike of small flowers.

As the flopsy bunnies discovered, lettuce is very soporific.

The latex or sap contains chemicals which help soothe restlessness, excitability and insomnia – it's a key ingredient in my sleep mix.

It can also be used to ease colic, painful periods and joint aches and pains.

Chamomile
Chamomilla recutita/Matricaria chamomilla

Chamomile is a very familiar herb and a member of the daisy family. There are many members of the daisy family, two are called chamomile:

1. German chamomile has lots of daisy-like flowers which look like shuttlecocks with the white petals (ray florets) appearing to grow backwards and the yellow hollow centre (disc florets), with fine leaves. The aroma is very fragrant and this is used in the chamomile tea that can be bought easily in tea bags or as a loose tea.

2. Roman chamomile has flowers with many more white petals and denser clumps of fine leaves, and a much sharper fragrance – if you make a tea out of it you will have a very bitter drink.

Although they are used interchangeably for their relaxing effect on the nervous system and, because they are both quite bitter, they have a beneficial effect on the digestive system. I use German chamomile in my sleep mix and Roman chamomile in my IBS mixture – the extra bitterness is an advantage in digestive tonics.

Some people require a soothing cream with a healing element and I prescribe chamomile cream for them – it produces tiny amounts of a blue oil called chamazulene – which is an oil that encourages wound healing.

Memory

Ginkgo
Ginkgo biloba

Ginkgo is one of the oldest tree species and a tree which probably would not be here now except that the ancient Chinese took a fancy to it and many specimens were introduced into their parks and gardens about 3000 years ago. During this process they discovered that it had some very useful health benefits. Ginkgo's high tolerance for air pollution makes it an excellent tree for bringing greenery into cities; it is currently one of the most prolific street trees globally. I don't recommend making a tea from their leaves as the lower air quality in cities may well undermine its medicinal properties.

There was a theory among some herbalists that the best way to discover the beneficial uses of a herb was to look at it and see which part of the body it most resembled – 'The Doctrine of Signatures'. In the case of ginkgo – half a brain. Neatly, gingko is very beneficial for brain function – the theory didn't always work out as well in other cases and the principle was abandoned in favour of empirical knowledge and clinical trials.

Ginkgo increases the circulation of oxygenated blood to the brain thereby improving memory and brain function in general. Crucially it does this without increasing blood pressure which makes ginkgo ideal for treating mild memory loss or early stage dementia in older people, who often have high blood pressure. Ginkgo also has blood thinning properties; one of the major contraindications for taking ginkgo as a supplement/medicine is that it can interact with warfarin – a powerful blood thinner – potentially making the blood too 'thin' thereby affecting its ability to clot, which makes it hard to stop an injury from bleeding.

I have a patient who suffered a pulmonary embolism – a tiny blood clot had become stuck in one of the capillaries in her lung, causing sudden onset breathlessness – the area of lung beyond the clot could no longer function. She went to A&E and was given blood thinners to dissolve the clot – this was very effective and she went home with a prescription for warfarin. After a while she became uneasy about taking such a strong drug long term and we had a discussion about replacing it with ginkgo. Her GP was happy for her to try a gradual replacement of warfarin with a fluid extract; three or four times stronger than a standard tincture of gingko, with regular blood tests to ensure that her blood clotting ability remained within the prescribed guidelines. This has proved very effective over the years and she has not had any side effects to contend with. Clearly this could only be done with the support of her GP and is certainly not something to do at home.

Ginkgo also helps ease the symptoms of asthma by reducing airway inflammation.

Rosemary
Rosmarinus officinalis

Rosemary is another escapee from the Mediterranean
– it enjoys direct sunlight and well drained soils –
generally it flowers early in spring.

I was told about a large specimen near one of the
University buildings in Liverpool. It's not large, it's
huge – so big that you can walk past it assuming that it
can't be rosemary because of its size. It was there 26
years ago; I don't know if it's still there – the sheltered
position obviously suited it down to the ground.

Very fragrant, it contains essential oils that improve
the circulation of blood to the head and are very
uplifting. I have a patient with a heart condition and,
although hawthorn was doing a great job, my patient
was feeling tired. When I added rosemary to his
mixture he felt more energetic and awake but in a
sustainable way. A gentle tonic.

Rosemary is good for the memory and for improving
hair growth – as long as there is hair present to start
with – it's not 'miracle grow'.

Lemon Balm
Melissa officianalis

A member of the labiate family, it has similar habits to mint including spreading everywhere in the garden. It is a beautiful spring green plant with a refreshing lemony scent and tiny white flowers.

As a tea it is relaxing and uplifting. As a tincture it is quite different – very dark and rich but usually without a hint of lemon. The volatile oil is only found in small quantities within the plant – it takes a huge amount of lemon balm plants to extract a small amount of the essential oil.

This herb is a useful liver tonic and is a gentle nervine (it supports the nervous system); a nice cup of lemon balm tea after a difficult day is a good way to ease tension and it aids sleep too.

Lemon balm tincture has anti-viral properties – particularly useful for treating cold sores – dab a little of the tincture on to the affected area at the first 'tingle' or suggestion that a cold sore may erupt and this should prevent it developing.

Some years ago, Newcastle University did some research on four herbs that might help improve memory.

A group of massage therapists were asked to massage the hands of volunteers who were residents of retirement homes – their memories were tested before and after a preselected number of massages and for those massaged with lemon balm their cognitive ability had improved significantly.

Wood Betony
Stachys betonica

A summer herb that grows among the grass sometimes
along with St John's wort – they seem to be friends,
which is nice. Wood betony has a few leaves, a tallish
stem at 6"- 8", and a tightly packed bundle of pink
flowers at the top.

It's the flowers and leaves that are used – I have said
many times (much to the amazement of others) that I
think that a tincture made from wood betony smells
like strawberries. OK, maybe a little farfetched but it
certainly has a fruity aroma.

This herb has an affinity for the head and the
nervous system – headaches are often treated with
wood betony especially if they are associated with
tension. I use it with people who want to improve their
memory – I combine it with ginkgo and it improves the
circulation to the head without increasing blood
pressure, helping with clear thinking and memory.

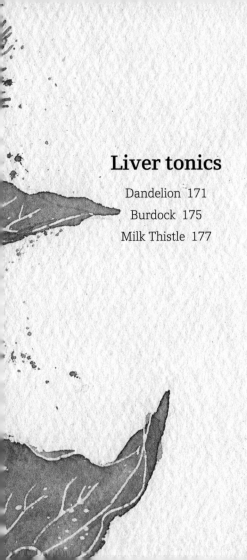

Liver tonics

Dandelion root and leaf
Taraxacum officinale

Dandelion flowers are bright yellow and make you smile.

Dandelion root is very effective at detoxifying the liver and is a key ingredient in my liver mix formula. It's always easy to underestimate anything that seems common or 'easy to come by' and dandelions fall into this category.

A number of times over the years I've had patients who have had liver function tests that show that they have raised enzymes or even – on a couple of occasions – early signs of cirrhosis. Dandelion root is excellent at removing any toxins present or at least reducing the toxic load in the liver especially if it's combined with a small amount of burdock root. Milk thistle is the herb to heal the liver once the dandelion root has done its work. This combination has proved time and again to be very effective – most recently a patient was told that she had signs of a fatty liver one summer, and by autumn a follow up test showed that her liver enzymes were back within the normal range.

That's another thing that happens with herbs – we can underestimate how quickly they can work.

Dandelion leaves are an excellent diuretic, particularly because they contain high levels of potassium. When someone takes a diuretic they will lose potassium as well as the excess fluid, which can lead to problems associated with potassium deficiency. Due to the high levels of potassium in dandelion leaves this deficiency very, very rarely occurs and they are a really effective diuretic.

Water retention can happen for a number of reasons, the main one is heart failure. Fluid seeps into the surrounding tissues causing oedema. The herbs to treat this condition are mainly a selection of the herbs for the heart that have already been mentioned but dandelion leaves may also be included in the mixture.

Sometimes we don't know why we retain fluid – maybe it's because the weather is hot or we have been sitting for a long time – this is the type of fluid retention that dandelion leaves treat very effectively.

One patient in her 80s had suffered swollen ankles since she had her second child over 50 years previously – a simple mixture (taking other health issues into consideration) mainly consisting of dandelion leaves – gave her back her ankles. She only needed the mixture for four months before her body rebalanced itself.

Burdock
Arctium lappa

This herb has big leaves and grows exactly where it wants to grow – even in the middle of the road. It has a very long root, purple thistle like flowers which turn into vicious sticky burrs.

Burdock root is an ingredient in the liver mix I make up for people whose livers could do with a bit of extra support. I use it in small quantities because it really digs deep and shifts stuff. In my early days as a Medical Herbalist I gave burdock root to someone with eczema on her hands (skin conditions can be associated with a congested liver) – after only two weeks it had reached her elbows! Too much burdock can cause the liver to detoxify too quickly and can make things worse before they get better. Herbalists are not infallible and I've tried to learn from this experience so as not to put anyone else through such a dramatic 'healing crisis'.

Milk Thistle
Carduus marianus

A thistle with a white milky pattern on its green leaves.

This is such a healing herb for the liver and it also offers significant protection. The majority of milk thistle is grown in America where young people will drink a milk thistle seed mixture before going out for the night to avoid a hangover the next day – I understand that it's very effective.

As I've already mentioned, the healing effects of this herb on the liver are very impressive (see 'dandelion root'). It's healing effect on the liver can be very profound when used in conjunction with a change of diet and lifestyle.

Menopause

St John's Wort
Hypericum perforatum

This herb grows in open grassy areas; it's about eight inches high and has many yellow flowers. It flowers throughout the summer – each plant will have buds, seed heads and flowers at the same time.

There are many varieties of St John's wort but only *hypericum perforatum* has the healing properties that I am about to describe. This plant can be identified by holding a leaf up and looking 'through it'. If you see some black dots which leave a purple smear on your finger if you rub the leaf you have the correct variety.

St John's wort has a reputation for relieving mild to moderate depression; it is also a useful anti-inflammatory and has useful anti-viral properties.

One of the first patients that I saw after qualifying had mysterious aches and pains – she had not had a diagnosis from a doctor but she had been offered anti-inflammatories which she was reluctant to take. Her muscle pains were never given a definitive diagnosis because after taking a herbal mixture mainly consisting of St John's wort, the inflammation resolved and as far as I know has never returned. For a long time after this I used to tell people that treating mysterious aches and pains was a lot easier than treating rheumatoid arthritis – which often presents as mysterious aches and pains. Since then, I've spent time with some very skilled herbalists and have borrowed some of their ideas for treating osteo and rheumatoid arthritis. Much to the relief of my patients!

I find that *hypericum* is very helpful in easing the emotional rollercoaster known as the menopause: A woman came to see me as a patient and started the consultation with the words 'My husband said as I was leaving the house "Why are you going to see a herbalist when we should be going to marriage counselling?" I asked why he said this and she replied 'Because I want to kill my family'. I was also beginning to wonder if she had come to see the right person. As the consultation progressed, I realised that she was going through a particularly difficult menopause. The menopause is a time when physical health problems need to be taken seriously and it can cause personality changes as well. The change in hormone levels is hardly noticed by some women and for others these changes can cause anxiety, mood swings, night sweats, hot flushes, loss of confidence, memory lapses and vaginal dryness to name but a few. I decided to start with a simple approach – a blend of wild yam cream (this is considered controversial by some; I find it evens out hormonal fluctuations and doesn't have to be used for very long) with St John's wort tincture. Two weeks later this patient came back smiling saying that she quite liked her family and was glad that she hadn't done anything rash.

If the flowers – which are yellow – are placed in a clear glass jar with sunflower oil and exposed to sunlight for a few weeks, the oil becomes an iridescent red colour, which is found in the tiny oil glands in the petals and top leaves extracted by the UV light in sunlight. This oil is a powerful anti-inflammatory and reduces pain when it is applied externally. I have had many patients use this oil on longstanding injuries and they have been able to reduce or stop taking painkillers as a result.

Another patient had an ulcer on her leg which wasn't responding to treatment, she applied *calendula* and *hypericum* oils to the area, it healed with barely a scar.

Rose
Rosa damascena

Roses probably originated in the Middle East, and have been admired for their colour and fragrance throughout history. Damascus roses are particularly fragrant because they are grown at a high altitude.

When I was teaching at the herbal clinic in Preston the students used to call rose tincture a 'hug in a bottle'; anyone who seemed lonely would get a small amount included in their mixture.

I use rose tincture and rose aromatic water which is a by–product of rose oil distillation. I find it to be particularly effective in cooling hot flushes and night sweats in menopausal women. It is also very effective in treating vaginal dryness – another joy of the menopause. Roses are cooling and moisturising, and smell pretty good as well. Rose cream is an excellent moisturiser and has a toning effect on mature skin.

Ladies Mantle
Alchemilla vulgaris

Ladies mantle has very furry leaves with irregular edges which hold rain drops long after they have evaporated from other leaves. It produces an abundance of small yellow flowers.

Ladies mantle is traditionally a woman's herb – it's quite astringent which helps reduce the flow of heavy periods and it also eases the pain that can be associated with them. During the menopause, when periods can become heavy, this herb helps regulate the flow.

It is also a useful remedy for treating diarrhoea – in men as well as women.

A valuable herb that I often recommend to be taken as a tea, as required.

Red Clover
Trifolium pratense

Red clover flowers are generally large and if you pick them – away from roads and dogs – you can pull the petals out and suck the ends for a small sugar hit.

I often recommend red clover tea – it soothes irritated skin conditions (particularly in children), moistens mucous membranes and eases coughs, and also reduces hot flushes due to the presence of phytooestrogens.

Something for everyone.

Adrenal support

Borage
Borago officinalis

A relative of comfrey, the flowers range from blue to pink – the flowers are so beautiful that they have been included in ice cubes and added to the drink Pimms – although this isn't obligatory.

Top leaves and flowers are the parts used.

I use this herb a lot – the tincture has a nourishing effect on the adrenal glands – these are pyramid shaped structures on top of the kidneys. Three catecholamines are produced and stored here – dopamine (increases cardiac output and flow of blood to the kidneys) – norepinephrine and epinephrine (types of adrenalin) are released in response to extreme stress (the flight or fight response). We live in stressful times and if we suffer from chronic stress – stress that goes on for a long time – this depletes our adrenal glands which has the effect of causing the release of adrenalin inappropriately which can cause panic attacks and general anxiety.

Borage has a calming and restorative effect and if used with other herbs that support the nervous system it can be amazingly powerful and effective.

'Borage for courage'.

Liquorice
Glycyrrhiza glabra

This herb has the appearance of a pea-like shrub.

Liquorice is a member of the pea family and used to be imported into this country from Europe until someone discovered that it grew really well in Pontefract – where the industry making Pontefract cakes was born. The root is the part that is used; it is eight times sweeter than sugar and it is still possible to buy dried roots to chew, making it an alternative to jelly babies. If the root is boiled according to a secret recipe (I don't know what it is anyway) a black syrup is produced which can be used in confectionery or medicine.

In medieval times it was considered to be a moistening, soothing medicine and this is still true today. It is also an adrenal restorative; it may have its effect more quickly than borage which is a very gentle herb but there is a caution to using liquorice – it has the side effect of causing sodium to be retained within the body, due to this fluid-retention may occur – this combination can put your blood pressure up. Part of an initial consultation with me involves having your blood pressure taken – if your blood pressure is at the high end of normal or simply high then I will avoid prescribing liquorice.

Liquorice is anti-inflammatory, soothing mouth ulcers and stomach ulcers – it contains saponins which foam up similar to soap. They coat the stomach in a protective layer. Liquorice is also a key ingredient in cough syrups – it acts as a soothing 'expectorant' making coughs more productive and less painful.

Pain

Yellow Gentian
Gentiana lutea

Both the flower and the root are yellow.

The root is used – when it is dried it develops a particularly bitter flavour. This herb contains an element which has the strongest bittering that herbalists use.

Gentian is particularly good at stimulating appetite and is an excellent digestive tonic. If the liver is working efficiently prostaglandins, which are chemicals that form part of the pain pathway, are broken down quickly and the perception of pain is reduced.

Yellow Jasmine
Gelsemium sempervirens

Yellow jasmine or winter jasmine – the yellow flowers
are one of the earliest flowers to be seen in the year.
When the flowers are over, the leaves develop.

This is a Class 20 herb which means that it can only
be prescribed by a qualified herbalist.

The tincture has a local anaesthetic effect if it's
applied to the skin externally. If it's used in a mixture
the dose has to be very carefully monitored. A herbalist
friend of mine put together a mixture of gentian,
gelsemium and lavender which she gave to a patient of
hers who suffered from severe headaches. Not only did
it help ease the headaches, her patient also took the
mixture after a skiing accident to ease the pain – which
it did very effectively.

A side effect of taking *gelsemium* is that it can slow
your heart rate down and taking too much will cause
your heart to stop.

Lavender
Lavandula angustifolia

Lavender is a familiar fragrant herb, its flowers are very popular with bees. It will grow in Cumbria if the ground is well drained.

I struggle with prescribing lavender in a mixture because the taste and smell are more associated with room sprays and massage oils for me. I haven't met anyone else who has the same reservations so it must be something particular to me.

As I've described with the *gelsemium*, gentian and lavender mixture, lavender has a useful relaxing effect which complements the stronger herbs.

As well as being great for treating headaches, it's uplifting and helpful in treating mild depression, also aiding restful sleep – some people make pillows which they fill with dried lavender flowers; the fragrance helps them relax and get to sleep.

Willow
Salix alba

The flowering of willow is an early sign of spring –
catkins are a welcome sight after winter. Willow
branches are harvested in spring because it's easier to
strip the bark from them at this time of year. The bark
can be dried and used in a decoction, or used fresh or
dry in a tincture.

Willow is the starting point of aspirin – over
100 years ago a French pharmacist identified the
main chemical constituents in willow bark – salicin
and acetylsalicylic acid. Aspirin is made from
acetylsalicylic acid which is a good painkiller but
can irritate the stomach lining causing bleeding. The
combination of the acetylsalicylic acid and salicins
not only reduce the perception of pain due to blocking
the prostaglandin pathway but also have an anti-
inflammatory effect.

This effect helps people manage pain, particularly
that of rheumatoid and osteo arthritis, also headaches,
gout and period pain.

Willow bark also reduces fevers and thins blood.

Circulation

Horse Chestnut
Aesculus hippocastanum

Conkers are the familiar fruit of the horse chestnut tree; dark brown and shiny, they provide 'harmless' entertainment when a string is put through them and you take turns to hit your opponent's conker until one breaks – the unbroken conker being the winner. A game that has been played for what may well be centuries is now considered to have dangers attached to it and the wearing of safety glasses is encouraged in some schools – I'm not sure what type of conkers they are using.

If you chop up conkers and make a tincture out of them you end up with a mixture that looks like milky tea, and if you shake the bottle an impressive foam is produced. Horse chestnuts contain saponins which cause the mixture to foam.

The outer shell contains high levels of tannins which are astringent and as a whole the tincture has the effect of being a circulatory stimulant.

I use horse-chestnut tincture to treat varicose veins. It has the ability to strengthen the veins and improves the circulation. This herb is also often part of the treatment for haemorrhoids.

Yarrow
Achillea millefolium

Millefolium, meaning many flowers, has a flat white or pink flower head made up of multiple flowers with yellow centres.

Yarrow is a relative of chamomile – their similarities are that they both produce a bitter tea if left to stand for five-ten minutes. This encourages the production of bile which improves digestion, especially of fats.

Yarrow is excellent at improving circulation. I use it a lot in mixtures for people with high blood pressure – improved circulation drops the overall pressure in the body.

Yarrow also regulates the flow of periods – lightens heavy periods and increases the flow of light periods that don't quite 'get going'.

Particularly useful in the treatment of fibroids – growths that form in or around the uterus – a bath with a sock full or a muslin bag of yarrow reduces the heavy bleeding associated with fibroids.

Many years ago I had a patient with a thrombosis due to sitting in a plane for a considerable amount of time. A blood 'thinner' resolved the blood clot but thereafter his leg would ache at night – a cup of yarrow tea before bed improved the circulation in his leg and helped him sleep comfortably.

Another patient brought her new partner to see me as he had very cold hands. He was on a number of medications and had come to see me out of curiosity. I decided to go for a conservative treatment which was yarrow – in about a week I was reliably informed his hands had warmed up significantly.

My son had an outdoor/outward bound birthday party when he was 14; I didn't know about the old, unreliable penknife until I was shown a cut finger – the deadline was a cello lesson four hours later – for the rest of the party this boy had either a plantain or yarrow poultice on his finger which stopped the bleeding sufficiently. It wasn't a complete cure but not bad for woodland A&E.

Bilberry
Vaccinium myrtillus

Small purple berries found on low spreading shrubs on the fells.

Apparently during the Second World War fighter pilots were encouraged to eat bilberry jam – bilberries contain a chemical called visual purple which is important for night vision.

I use this berry to support people with cataracts or other problems with their vision – brightly coloured or deep purple fruits or vegetables contain leutine which is important for eye health.

Bilberries help balance blood sugar and strengthen veins – which is helpful in the treatment of varicose veins.

Nervous system

Oats
Avena sativa

Oats are a hardy crop; they even grow as far north as Scotland and porridge is as good for you as they say. A source of soluble fibre it gives you energy as well.

A bag of oats suspended under the hot tap in the bath will produce a soothing, milky bath water which will ease the discomfort of eczema and other irritated skin conditions.

I use oats as a restorative for the nervous system – because it's nutritious as well as healing, this herb is ideal if someone is suffering from nervous exhaustion.

Skullcap
Scutellaria lateriflora

Skullcap is a member of the mint family and has similar habits, if it likes where it has been planted – it doesn't like my garden. It's low growing with tiny blue flowers.

It's a nervine, helping to relax the nervous system in people who are suffering from nervous exhaustion. I tend to use it alongside valerian – I find that valerian has an instant effect which gives the skullcap time to have its deeper, longer lasting effect. Over time it helps the nervous system to recover from chronic stress.

Vervain
Verbena officinalis

This herb has very fine spike of tiny pink flowers.

Another nervine, it combines well with skullcap because it is uplifting as well as having a calming effect.

When I went to an American herbal conference, amongst all the other valuable information that I picked up was a mixture to treat anxiety from David Winston. The talk was about the anxiety and depression that people who have had heart attacks often suffer. The mixture is made up of *verbena* for the overthinking aspect of anxiety, *rhodiola* as a calming tonic, and *polygala tenuifolia* for the anxiety. The beauty of this mixture is that it doesn't make you feel tired, just calmer and more able to cope.

In conclusion...

... the importance of old wives tales

I've really enjoyed jotting down my thoughts about some of the herbs that I use; including the stories to go with them has hopefully provided some context too.

I can say on the whole my patients are very patient with the idea that a thinly disguised version of their story is appearing in print, however I want to conclude this book with some stories that were relayed to me by two retired midwives – a glimpse of times passed yet also within living memory.

Evelyn Jenkins 1934 – 2017
Jean Docherty 1935 – 2019

Jean was Northern Irish or Scottish Irish and Evelyn was Welsh – they trained and worked with quite a number of nurses over the years, sharing houses to reduce costs. As time went by, the other nurses left to get married or work elsewhere ultimately leaving Jean and Evelyn together in Barrow-in-Furness. At this point they decided that they got on well enough to buy a house together and enjoy retirement. They provided somewhere safe and dry for local school children to stay after school hours if their parents were delayed for any reason.

When I met Jean and Evelyn their kindness was being repaid by their neighbours calling in to see that they were OK and doing odd jobs for them – although it slightly baffled Evelyn and Jean; after all they had done nothing special as far as they could see. Their kindness did mean a lot to those around them.

Evelyn, as quite a small child, asked her mother for some paper and a pencil; she went to sit at the table and quietly got on with drawing a picture of her father's boots – no one suspected that she could draw until this moment. The drawing was on the wall at school for what to Evelyn was an embarrassingly long time – being very modest. After her local schooling she studied art in London, receiving a fine arts degree before deciding that she wanted to do something that she could see would help people and so she trained as a nurse. She managed to get through postmortems by drawing everything that she saw in great detail. Jean used to say that taking over a shift from Evelyn was a pleasure – everything was written down, clearly too! Unusually for the times, Evelyn always asked you to sit while she went through each patient and their treatment history. At one point in her nursing career, she was called into a consultant's office; they were overheard by Jean and a West Indian nurse as he said to Evelyn "You're too clever to be a nurse, I think that you should train to be a doctor." (this was in the 1940s); Evelyn replied that

God wanted her to be a nurse and that was what she
would continue to do. Jean and the West Indian nurse
turned to one another and wondered "Would anyone
say that to them?". They didn't think so.

Jean was one of nine children, so whereas Evelyn
was quiet and self-effacing, Jean could, and would,
tell a story. Almost all I know about Evelyn comes
from Jean.

One evening Jean's mother was wondering if she
had indigestion when the penny dropped that she
was not only pregnant but going into labour – she
mentioned this to Jean's father who disappeared from
view behind the newspaper that he was reading. The
doctor was called and eventually a scrawny four pound
baby was delivered and put to one side because Mrs
Docherty was seriously ill – later she would tell Jean
that she prayed that if only one of them could live
to let it be her, as she explained she had eight other
children who needed her. She asked Jean what she
thought of her, not wanting to save her latest child
at the cost of her own life – Jean was very pragmatic
and said that it was obvious to hope that her mother,
at least, would live. The following morning someone
picked up the baby intending to arrange for it to be
buried and noticed that she was breathing – Jean was
passed to her mother who was thankfully somewhat
rested and out of danger; she suckled furiously. The

Doctor had a word with Mr Docherty telling him in no uncertain terms that Mrs Docherty's life was not to be put in danger again by putting her through another pregnancy. According to Jean her mother was 60 at the time.

They were very poor and only survived because Mr Docherty was so good at growing potatoes. He died when Jean was nine years old.

Her mother lived into her eighties and was a very pious woman whose belief and trust in God helped her through some very difficult times. Jean recalled that 'If she promised you a penny you would be given a penny, and if you had been naughty and were promised a slap you would get a slap' – even if you had run away and hidden for hours hoping she would forget – she never forgot.

From a young age Jean was fascinated by animals; around the time she was five she would stay with the local vet and his wife, going out on calls with him, both of them riding on the vet's pony. She particularly enjoyed going out on calls at night – they were particularly exciting. Jean mused that "It wouldn't be allowed now" and she's right; health and safety and the possibilities of child abuse would prevent a child from spending so much time away from family. Also, not many vets would want a five-year-old trailing after them. Although she really enjoyed being with the animals and seeing them being treated, she felt that she wasn't clever enough to be a vet and decided instead to become a nurse (interestingly).

When Jean was about 16 she developed a rash on her neck; she had very long hair which was difficult to wash – it took a couple of brothers or sisters to help her. On one occasion the rash was noticed and treated at home by Mrs Docherty – to no avail. Eventually she went to see the doctor who arranged for her to be treated with radium at the Belfast Hospital – after a couple of treatments she told the nurse in charge that she thought that she'd had enough treatments because the rash had gone. She was told in no uncertain terms that the doctor would decide when she had received sufficient treatments and that it was not up to her.

Jean was slim at 16 but after the radium treatments she began to put on weight – this became an issue for her all her life, although at least one fellow Irish compatriot told her that they were all big people where they came from.

Radium does seem to be a powerful treatment for a rash – perhaps there was some level of experimenting involved.

In her late teens Jean left Northern Ireland to train to be a nurse in England. As a student nurse she and another student were allocated a patient with an infected leg. Every morning they would have to un-bandage the man's leg and scrape out the pus and infected tissue – the man was in agony. After several of these mornings Jean thought to herself "What would my mother do?" She would apply a bread poultice – so Jean went to the ward kitchen and boiled up some bread with water and salt (her mother would have used bicarbonate of soda). When it had dissolved into a hot mush, she wrapped it in a sterile dressing and applied it to the infected leg – she kept it in place for several hours and a large amount of foul-smelling green 'matter' came out. The patient and Jean were very impressed; she even took a swab of the 'matter' in case it was considered necessary to culture any bacteria present. This was at a time before antibiotics were easily available.

The next day the patient's room was filled with people in white coats and when Jean appeared her patient saw her and said "That's her, she healed my leg". His leg was pink and healthy so when the senior clinician asked her to join him for a quiet word, she was totally unprepared for his stern warning to 'never do anything like this again'. Apparently healing patients was not the important thing, the important thing was to follow approved procedure whether the patient recovered or not.

Jean and Evelyn worked in many hospitals over many years throughout the country, and both of them were surprised that they had ended up being midwives.

I have used bread poultices over the years, on myself and even George, my dog; they are an effective way of drawing pus/matter out of a cyst or boil.

Although I haven't recommended it for my patients to try, it's there in the back of my mind as an old wives tale that has saved at least one life. A lot of the herbal lore is based on old wives tales. It's good to remember that old wives and their tales should never be underestimated.

Jean and Evelyn were devout Christians which provided them both with great support and comfort. I consider myself more of a floating voter – I'm not convinced wholly by any orthodox religion. I don't think that this matters, what matters is that I believe in something – a deity, Gaia or an un-named higher power or source. I find this reassuring. We need to look after the planet and the people – one can't happen without the other. I think what I'm trying to say is that if we respect ourselves, other people, all the flora and fauna, and learn from the past, then I think that the planet will allow us to stay for a bit longer.

Thank you for taking the time to read this collection of tales from the hedgerow, I hope you find them as intriguing as I do;

Sarah Atkinson March 2021

Index of herbs ~ common name

Index of herbs ~ latin name

The author
and the artist

Sarah Atkinson, MNIMH Dip.Phyt.

Sarah is a Medical Herbalist; she focuses on what we eat and drink combined with listening to people's life stories, which makes for a much more holistic approach to dis-ease.

www.medicine-garden.com

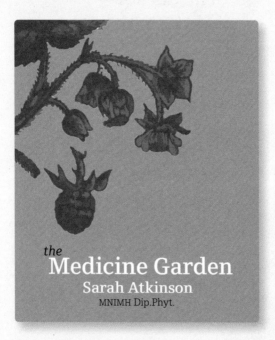

the **Medicine Garden**
Sarah Atkinson
MNIMH Dip.Phyt.

Sally Bamber, BA Hons Chelsea School of Art

Sally is a Graphic Designer and Artist; her focus is on arts-based design projects. She loves charcoal, paints flowers in watercolour and portraits in oil.

www.sallybamber.com

Sarah

When I was training at the School of Phytotherapy
(1989 – 1993) Hein Zeylstra, the principal of the school,
used to entertain us with his stories of herbal triumphs,
often concluding a story with the words 'and they were
completely cured'. My stories don't always end this way.

I qualified as a Medical Herbalist in 1993 and set up
my practice shortly afterwards. Initially I was seeing
patients from home just outside Liverpool but due to
family circumstances and small children I soon moved
to Cumbria and I have been in practice here for nearly
30 years. In 2006 I was able to set up my own clinic –
The Medicine Garden – in Ulverston. From this time I
have been doing regular herb walks each spring.

The way that I remember information is to attach it to
a story; my herb walks involve a collection of medicinal
herbs strung together by a selection of facts. Eventually
it occurred to me that I could write some of these stories
down and luckily for me Sally Bamber (local and
international watercolour artist specialising in plant
illustrations) has agreed to illustrate hese herbs for me.

Some of these herbs are not found in the Cumbrian
hedgerows and although originally this was going to be
a herb identification book to take with you on country
walks, it has now evolved into herbs that I know and love
– most of which can be found in and around Cumbria.

When we were all shut down and self-isolating during
the coronavirus, I found it difficult to buy herbs –
obviously the virus created a big demand for herbs that

can support the immune system, manage symptoms and aid convalescence; this situation made me look around and see how much was available for me to use even in my garden. I couldn't buy cough syrup but I could make it and, with some help from my son who also suddenly had a lot of spare time, I made a delicious wild cherry syrup. I have found it very interesting to see how many herbs I buy because I don't have time to make the tinctures myself but during lockdown I have found plenty of time to make a large variety of new tinctures from the herbs that grow around me.

I think that it's also worth mentioning that this is not an instruction book; it's more for your entertainment and interest – some of the stories involve herbs that should not be used by anyone who is not a qualified herbalist.

I have divided the herbs into groups for treating particular conditions but you will notice that all the herbs have more than one beneficial effect. Herbalists often use the same herb for different conditions or reasons. The groupings I have placed the herbs in reflect how I use these herbs.

Sarah Atkinson

www.medicine-garden.com
Sarah Atkinson
MNIMH Dip.Phyt.

Sally

In 2008 we arrived in Cumbria to live. I was painting portraits in oil. I set about my first exhibition working in partnership with Jo McGrath, her drawings of animals are alive and beautiful. 'The Two of Us' was an exhibition of 10 sitters and their animals; we asked our human sitters to add a statement about their connection with their animals. This exhibition then transferred to Farfield Mill, where we added two more sitters. In 2009 and 2013 I was lucky enough to have portraits accepted to the Lake Artists Society Summer Exhibition in Grasmere.

I was painting in our garage and found that the winter months became too cold to paint comfortably, so I moved into the kitchen and took up watercolour; it can take up less room and be simpler to put away. We then built a studio onto the house with fabulous views across the Duddon. I continued with the watercolours, using the garden as my subject – I would go out to pick a flower, bring it in and paint.

In 2013 I put together a proposal for Brantwood: to paint a new body of work of the flowers at Brantwood. Initially the prospect was daunting, then Sally Beamish, head gardener at Brantwood, offered a suggestion that resonated with me – Sally had been working on a wild flower meadow showing respect for local tradition fused with practical science, philosophy and spirituality for a holistic management style. Over the next two years you could often find me in the gardens, in the meadow, sat below the oak on Coniston Water's edge or tucked beneath

the wall in the tall growth at the edge of the meadow.
I was in my element. It amused me when my husband
described what I was doing; "she's painting weeds!"

From this exhibition I created two publications, both
are out of print having sold out. One was a 200 page A6
catalogue, the other an 20 page A3 display book. This
A3 book was significant because during the process of
drawing the flowers at Brantwood, the date and place
became important, adding a couple of lines about the
mood and place at the time of each drawing. I approached
Sarah Atkinson to ask if she would be interested in adding
some plant anecdotes that she would be happy for me to
publish. Happily she said yes! Sarah also recommended
that I ask Jane Alexander, Energy Practitioner and
Soul Worker and Teacher, if she would be interested in
contributing. Jane came and spent an afternoon with me
in the Hortus Inclusus at Brantwood. Three days later
she sent me 15 A4 pages that caused a mindshift for me.

In 2018 Sarah and I launched Sarah's first book, a
fascinating look at the history of herbs, 'A Window on
Medieval Medicine'. So this book; 'Herbal Chronicles' is
her second, mine too! This is a compilation of some of
what captivates us.

Sally Bamber

www.sallybamber.com
Sally Bamber
BA Hons Chelsea School of Art